DOOR J'ADORE

DOOR J'ADORE

A CELEBRATION OF THE WORLD'S MOST BEAUTIFUL DOORS

NICK ROWELL

RYLAND PETERS & SMALL
LONDON • NEW YORK

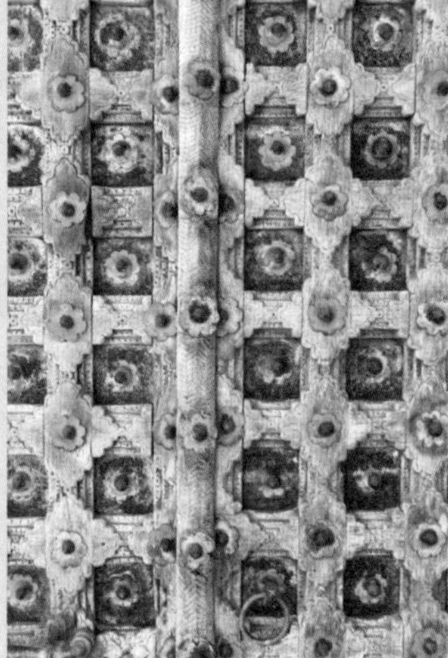

Senior designer Toni Kay
Senior commissioning editor Annabel Morgan
Picture research Christina Borsi
Head of production Patricia Harrington
Art director Leslie Harrington
Editorial director Julia Charles
Publisher Cindy Richards

First published in 2018 by
Ryland Peters & Small
20–21 Jockey's Fields,
London WC1R 4BW
and
341 East 116th Street
New York, NY 10029

www.rylandpeters.com

10 9 8 7 6 5 4 3 2 1

ISBN 978-1-84975-963-2

A CIP record for this book is
available from the British Library.

Library of Congress CIP data has
been applied for.

Printed and bound in China

"There are things known and there are things unknown, and in between there are doors." **ALDOUS HUXLEY**

FOREWORD

I never used to care much for doors. They were objects that I opened and closed; whether my own front door, or someone else's, they were merely functional barriers. Sometimes I might notice one that was more nicely kept than another, with a glossy paint job or roses scrambling round the door, but most of the time they were just things – things I needed to open, get through and close.

Then in 2008, my mum came to visit me in Buenos Aires. We would walk up and down the cobbled streets of the old San Telmo market looking at the antiques and silver while eyeing up the latest Tango partnerships on the street corners. One day mum was lagging behind, so I walked ahead to find somewhere for lunch. When she finally caught up, she showed me a picture of a door. At first I dismissed it, irritated because I was hungry, but she insisted on pointing out the details. 'Look at all the carving– it must have taken months to do,' she said, as I tried to flag down a waiter. I let her ramble on until I was tucking into dessert, at which point I started paying attention. She explained how grand the door was, how much history it carried, and how many stories it could tell, how many people it had let in and out, how many secrets it held – in short, that door was beautiful.

I wouldn't say it was exactly a eureka moment, but that day made me realize how little attention I had paid to doors in the past. Now I was drawn to their craftsmanship and the statements they were capable of making. Mum and I spent the following days snapping away, capturing every interesting door we saw. We even started varying our routes to walk through areas where we might find some good doors – it was like a treasure hunt, and we found treasure every time.

Nowadays, even a stroll to the supermarket is something of a door hunt for me. On weekends, I walk around London with friends, alert and ready for a corker. It's exciting because you never know where you'll end up – we have discovered all sorts of hidden corners as well as some truly wonderful doors.

INTRODUCTION

I don't claim to be a door expert (I'm not even sure that such a thing exists). But I've looked at a lot of doors over the past five years or so, and I'd like to share what I've noticed about them.

There are billions of doors around the world and, just like people, each one is different. Whether it's the shade of paint, the patina or texture of the finish, an extravagant brass knocker or an elegantly turned handle, every door reveals its past, its present, its culture and the person who lives behind it.

Doors are the portal between private and public. And therein lies their sense of mystery: without opening them we never know what or who lies behind them. Curiousity leads us to wonder what is beyond, and we only have what we see in front of us to go by, but take a closer look and you will find that every door tells its own story.

For example, the doors of the Greek island of Santorini, most of them painted an unassuming blue and surrounded by cascading bougainvillea, often hint at expansive views just beyond and a quick peek over a side wall may give an unexpected glimpse of the sea glittering in the distance. With the island in bloom almost all year round, the floral embellishments around Santorini's doors seem to symbolize the warm nature of the island's inhabitants and welcome us to the vibrant local culture.

In contrast, Moroccan doors present a closed face to the world. Massive in stature, their wood and iron panels studded with bolts and framed between unclimbable walls, these doors are seemingly impenetrable yet have their own story to tell. Like Indian doors, they are made using traditional techniques and the quality of the craftsmanship is remarkable, making these doors pieces of art in their own right. They are testament to the historic artisan culture in Morocco, which combines Berber traditions with Islamic, Jewish and European influences. If door guides existed, they wouldn't run out of stops when leading tourists around the old town of Fez or the souks of Marrakesh.

In vibrant cities such as Berlin or San Francisco, doors often serve as a canvas for self-expression or reflect popular culture. Some of the world's best street art and graffiti can be found in such cities, revealing political preoccupations and current trends. An example of this, albeit on a smaller scale, can be seen in the city of Funchal on the Portuguese island of Madeira. The local community handed over the doors of more than 200 abandoned buildings around the town to local artists. The result is quite brilliant, an egalitarian pavement art gallery that has regenerated the area's appeal.

However, some of the most enchanting doors I've come across are less obvious in their appeal. Derelict and dilapidated doors have their own allure and there is often a strange beauty in decay. Unhinged, faded, abandoned, neglected: these doors have a picturesque nobility to them – they are still standing, putting their best face forward and waiting to be opened one more time.

PAGES 10–11 *Its simplicity is what we first notice about this Nepalese door. That and the luscious saturated hues of its paintwork and the sheet that hangs alongside, screening the window.*

ABOVE *A half-door in Santorini invites passers-by to take a quick peek.*

OPPOSITE *This Notting Hill door relies on a vibrant yellow hue for its friendly demeanour.*

54

875
WWW.FMLATRIBU.COM
CONTROL
MENTAL

PAGE 14 *Ice-cream shades and the bluest of skies in Santorini, Greece.*

PAGE 15 *The bold chevrons that cover this mosque in the Maldives even extend to the doors.*

OPPOSITE AND ABOVE *Buenos Aires was where I first discovered my passion for doors – a city filled with a youthful and passionate spirit that inevitably spills over onto its streets.*

THIS PAGE *A riot of lush wisteria in full bloom softens the haughty grandeur of this Parisian entrance.*

ABOVE *At a Brazilian coffee plantation, the original 19th-century front door is adorned by an elaborate escutcheon.*

OPPOSITE *Traditional split barn doors in the Cotswolds, UK.*

PAGE 22 *Faded, aged layers of paint on a door in Pisa, Italy.*

PAGE 23 *At first glance, this stripped London door looks like an Impressionist painting. It reveals so many past coats of paint that one can only hope the owner varnished it and left it as it is.*

THIS PAGE *Let sleeping dogs lie.*

OPPOSITE *With its missing original fanlight and gradually distintegrating door, one gets the feeling that this grand, rusticated Irish doorway has seen better days, despite the jaunty scarlet paintwork.*

ABOVE *Multiple squares and right angles create a cubist composition.*

439

277

PAGES 28–29 *On the magical little island of Burano, close to Venice, every house is painted a different vibrant shade.*

ABOVE AND OPPOSITE *White walls, blue doors and great cascades of bougainvillea all add up to one thing – a Greek island.*

11

2

PAGE 32 *Perhaps Number 11 may be a little down on its luck, but even dilapidated paintwork has its own peculiar charm.*

PAGE 33 *It can only be Lisbon. Traditional azulejo tiles are complemented by a door that's the colour of green ink.*

RIGHT *Remarkable hand-painted antique doors spotted for sale in Jaipur, India.*

1C
Maria Freitas
11

OPPOSITE *In 2010, in the city of Funchal on the Portuguese island of Madeira, José Maria Montero had a brainwave: to invite artists to paint the doors of abandoned buildings. More than 100 artists participated in the Arte Portas Abertas (Art of Open Doors) project. The brief was simple: pick a door and allow your creativity to run riot.*

THIS PAGE *A blocked-up doorway on a Portuguese side street has been decorated with hand-painted tiles depicting an orange tree heavy with fruit.*

OPPOSITE *It's often worth taking a closer look at a door in order to properly appreciate the intricacies of the decoration. On this Indian door, metal floral motifs create a colourful repeating pattern.*

THIS PAGE *Elaborate carvings surround this emerald green door in Jodhpur, India.*

OPPOSITE *What could be more tantalizing than a door left just slightly ajar to provide a glimpse of a hidden Cuban courtyard?*

ABOVE *A mysterious wall of phantom doorways surrounds a stout wooden door in the City Palace of Jaipur, India.*

PAGE 42 *A coral-coloured London door is perfectly complemented by an extravagant display of flamingo pink camellias, begging the question of which came first – the door colour or the flowers?*

PAGE 43 *This clearly labelled entrance has a robust, no-nonsense charm. You couldn't miss it if you tried.*

DINGLE
HORSE RIDING
PRIVATE

1

MAD

PAGES 44 AND 45 *Two bold images from the Arte Portas Abertas (Art of Open Doors) project in Funchal, Madeira. Both amateur and professional artists decorated more than 200 dilapidated and unloved doors using paint, clay, metal, ceramic tiles and even the keys to a computer keyboard.*

ABOVE *In Rajasthan, India, a traditional arched door stands out thanks to its colour, shape and detailing.*

OPPOSITE *In one of the many courtyards of the City Palace in Jaipur, India, are four of the grandest doors in the world, all facing each other, each one as impressive as its neighbour. Ancient hand-painted patterns frame the gold-plated doors and make for four of the most regal and fabulous entrances in the world.*

OPPOSITE AND ABOVE *The doors to these French country houses have an austere beauty that's softened by the pale gold of the walls and, in the case of the house opposite, the scrambling climber that frames the door.*

LEFT *The archetypal blue-painted Greek doors surrounded by a profusion of bougainvillea.*

ABOVE *Flowery wall art brightens everyone's day, Florida, USA.*

OPPOSITE *By their very nature something of a blank canvas, doors can present an opportunity for self-expression. This colourful hand-painted South American door makes a confident statement to the outside world.*

PAGES 54–55 *The beauty of decay, London.*

25

4

PAGE 56 *Sturdy, hard-working and functional – what more can you ask? A 'salt of the earth' kind of door.*

PAGE 57 *The inaccessibility of Venetian doors makes them things of mystery. Anyone who's ventured down the narrow, twisting waterways of this sublime city will know how much intrigue and history they hold.*

OPPOSITE AND ABOVE *Two more doors from Funchal's* Arte Portas Abertas *(Art of Open Doors) project. The painted doors have become something of a tourist attraction and what used to be a rundown neighbourhood is now bustling with cafés and tourists.*

140

PAGE 60 *A door within a door in Cuba.*

PAGE 61 *The peeling layers of paint and exposed stonework that frame this door give it unique visual appeal.*

ABOVE *Indian colour palettes are a constant inspiration.*

OPPOSITE *The blue tiles that surround this door are echoed in the matching blue squares painted onto it – a perfect example of how the context and background of a door can give it even more impact.*

OPPOSITE *A perfectly preserved Regency villa in County Wexford, Ireland still retains its original door and brass knocker.*

ABOVE *An imposing 18th-century doorway in rural Wiltshire, UK.*

PAGE 66 *A vibrant depiction of Peru's Inca citadel Machu Picchu covers door, walls and window frames and makes for a photogenic facade.*

PAGE 67 *These fishermen bringing in an impressively large catch of the day make reference to the nearby fish market in Funchal, Madeira.*

142

ABOVE *Traditional Tadelakt plaster walls surround these wooden doors in a Moroccan spa.*

OPPOSITE *This door in Marrakech, Morocco, is one of my favourites due to its layers of detail: the mosaics, the carved stone, the craftsmanship, the horseshoe arch. Every time I look, there's something new to see.*

PAGES 70–71 *This door in Bali clearly states its intention: to intimidate anyone even thinking about opening it.*

25
Süddeutsche Zeitung
DIARIO
New Art
IT'S LIFT-OFF
PEACHES
SECRETS
Ricardo
Silva
2015

OPPOSITE AND RIGHT *Two doors from Funchal's Arte Portas Abertas (Art of Open Doors) project, which have turned the city streets into an open-air gallery. "We are bringing art to people who never had the habit of visiting exhibitions or museums," says Roberto Macedo Alves, one of the artists who took part in the project.*

PAGE 74 *Above left: The pineapple is an international symbol of hospitality and welcome – very apt; Top right: These matching brass knockers have a curiously lifelike effect; Below left: a seahorse design at a coastal location; Below right: an imposing Baroque knocker.*

PAGE 75 *A ferocious visage stands guard over this door. Knock at your peril!*

10A

1

OPPOSITE *The tall, narrow frame of this Portuguese door draws the eye upwards and gives it an imposing, slightly formidable presence.*

ABOVE *This humble door makes its presence felt due to the strong contrast with the vibrant ochre walls and floor.*

PAGES 78 AND 79 *A glimpse into another world and intricate trompe l'oeil tiles in the city of Funchal, Madeira.*

2011

ABOVE *A beautifully framed internal door. The monochrome palette and layers of pattern surrounding this entrance are truly enchanting.*

OPPOSITE *Mythological creatures guard the door to the Iraqi Embassy in Amman, Jordan, which was inspired by the famous Ishtar Gate of Babylon.*

3c

OPPOSITE *A patriotic scheme in Stockholm, Sweden boasts the country's national colours in the shape of a blue door and yellow walls.*

ABOVE T*his faded door-turned-mini-cacti nursery was spotted on the sleepy island of Vis, Croatia.*

19

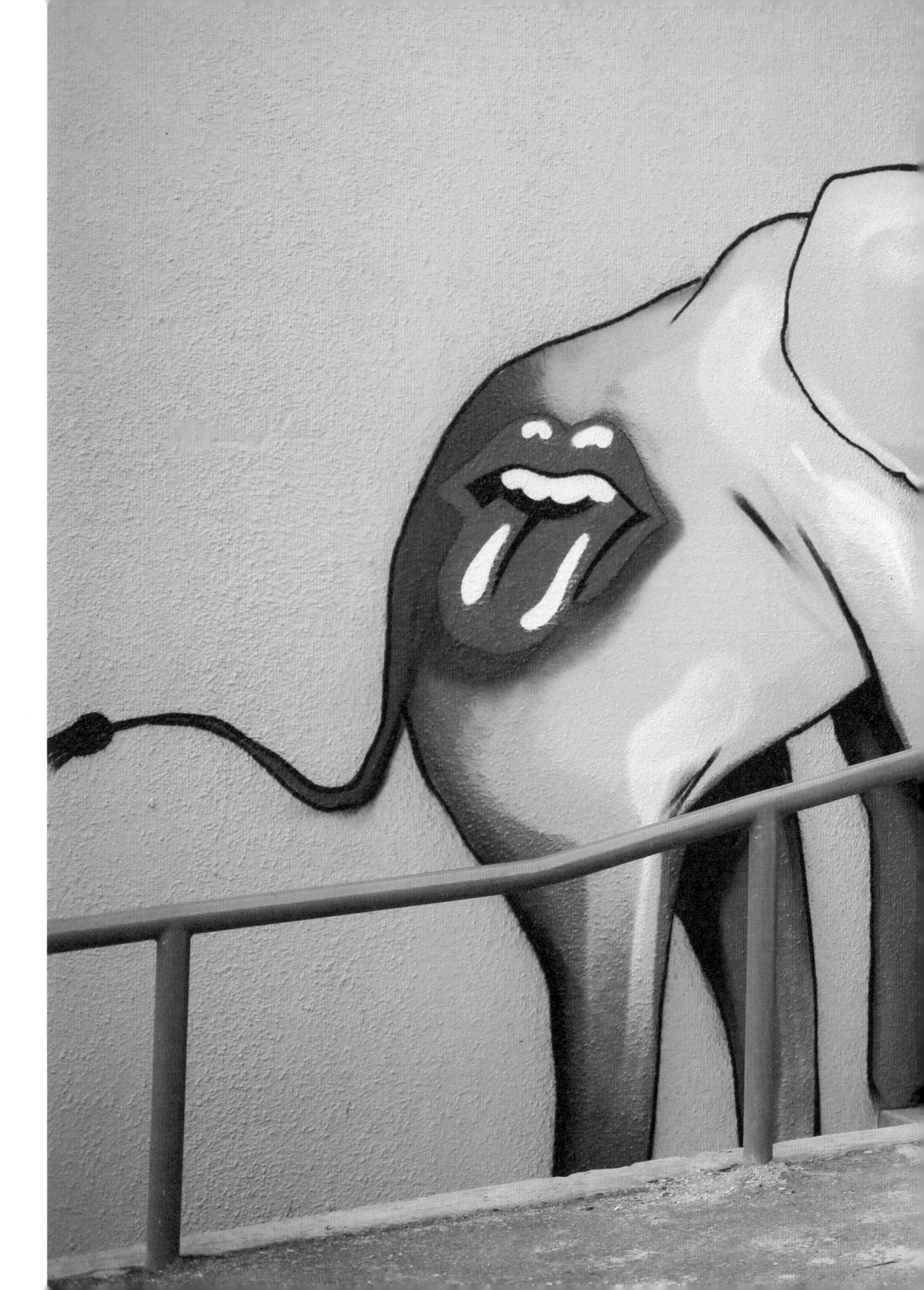

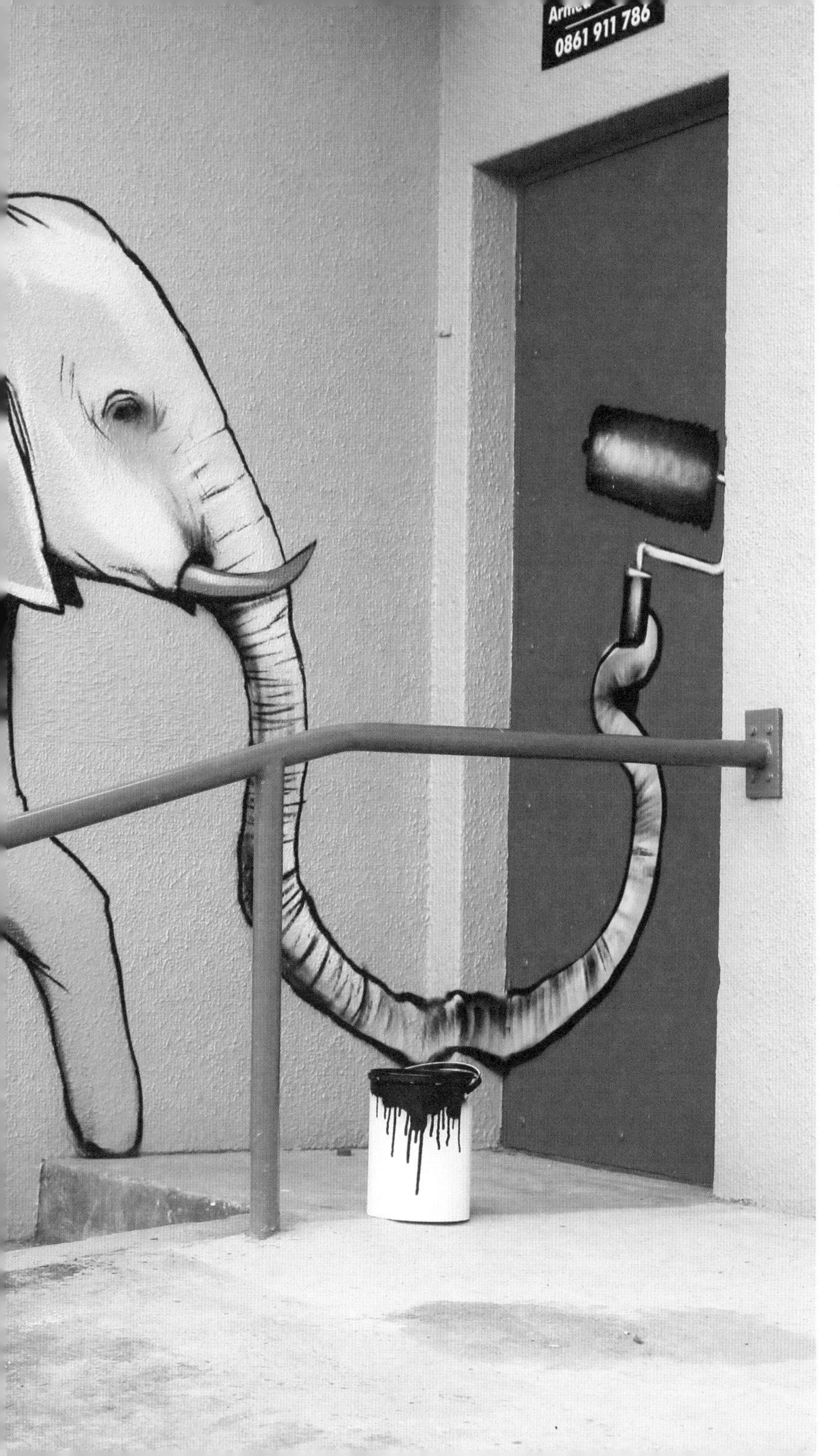

PAGES 84 AND 85 *Pretty as a picture: similar pastel schemes on the Isla di San Pietro, Carloforte, Sardinia and in the back streets of Marrakech, Morocco.*

LEFT *Falko One is one of South Africa's best-known and most celebrated graffiti artists. He often incorporates surrounding elements in his work and elephants are a recurrent theme.*

ABOVE AND OPPOSITE *Two sturdy handcrafted wooden doors, one in the rural south of France (above) and the other belonging to a traditional Karelian-style summerhouse on Lake Saimaa, Finland (opposite).*

PAGE 90 *This little Cuban casa is for sale. Who could resist the symmetrical façade, peppermint paintwork and ornate flourishes of the ironwork grille and door?*

PAGE 91 *More elaborate ironwork, this time teamed with bubblegum pink walls on a quiet back street in Italy.*

3

PAGES 92–93 *A slowly disintegrating shack is transformed into an artwork thanks to a door by South African street artist Falko One.*

ABOVE *You get the impression that this cottage door in St Ives, Cornwall, has seen it all over the years.*

OPPOSITE *Symmetrically studded doors and delicate mosaics in Chefchaouen, Morocco.*

8

OPPOSITE *Muted colours and intriguing textures lend an Italian door its understated appeal.*

ABOVE *This little faded pink number is tucked away in one of the romantic cobbled side streets that make Paris so charming.*

PAGES 98 AND 99 *Two doors from the Arte Portas Abertas (Art of Open Doors) project in Funchal, Madeira, which used the doors of empty properties as a canvas for public art. There are plans afoot to expand the project to other parts of Madeira and to mainland Portugal.*

181

O Jango

77

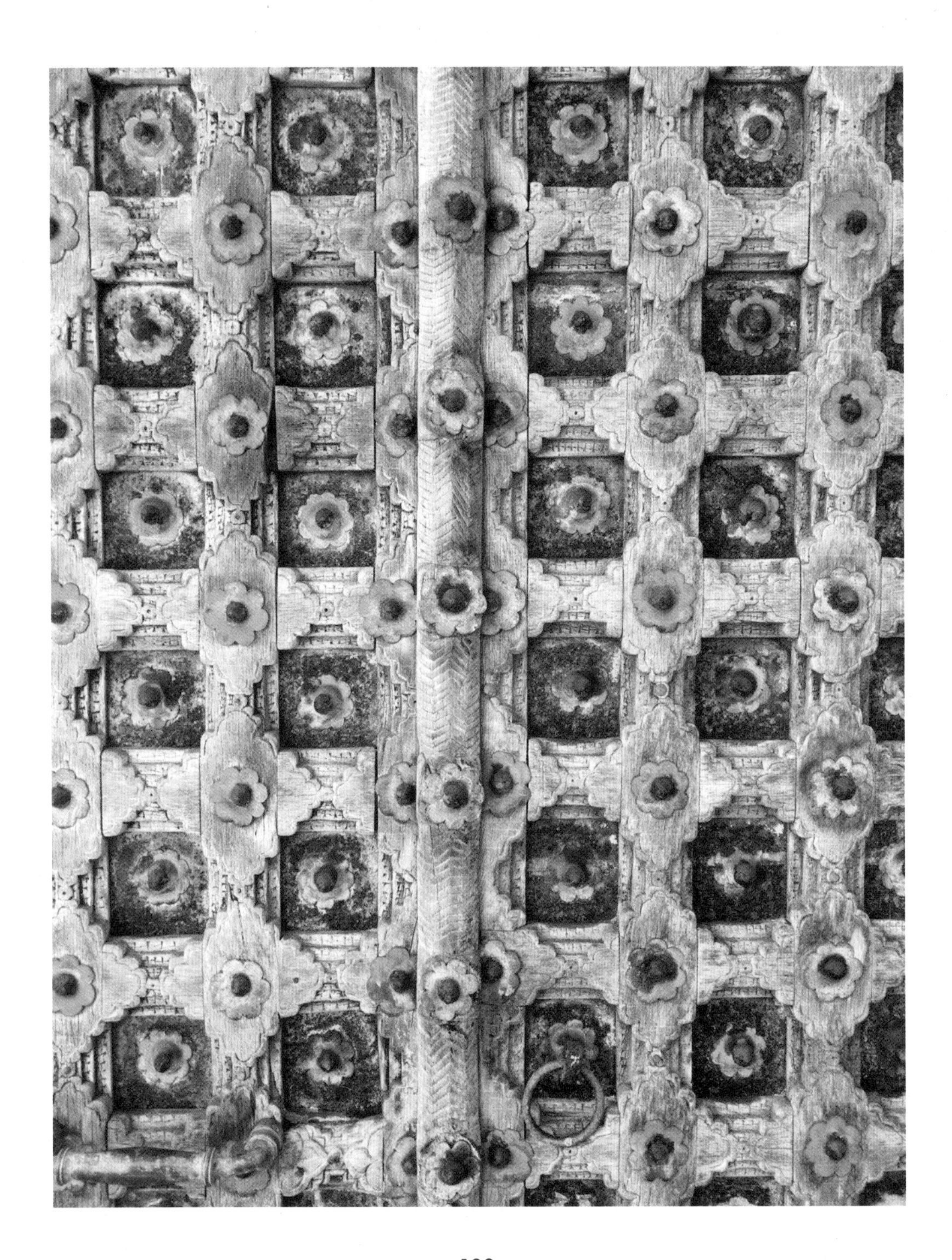

106
OFFICE &

PAGE 100 *This internal door studded with perfectly patinated bolts was spotted in Santiago, Chile.*

PAGE 101 *Some doors don't instantly catch the eye but reward a closer inspection. There's something soulful about this door's rich, saturated turquoise colour, the peeling layers of white paint around the doorway and the battle-scarred brickwork.*

RIGHT *You can't help but wonder about the story behind this romantic stage-set fantasy alongside a sober green door.*

ABOVE *Lisbon is famous for its traditional elaborately painted azulejo tiles, which clad many of the older buildings in the city.*

OPPOSITE *Overlapping scales and a faded green colourway give No.42 a slightly maritime vibe.*

PAGES 106 AND 107 *Angular carved frames and repeated floral motifs are common on Indian doors and are a sign of affluence and rank. It sometimes seems as if such doors are competing with each other for our attention and approval.*

42

VENDESI
RIVOLGERSI:
TEL.

THIS PAGE *'For Sale'. Let's hope the new owner is ready to sensitively restore this neglected facade to its former glory.*

ABOVE *The faded turquoise paint of this inviting entrance is accentuated by the detailed carved wooden frame.*

OPPOSITE *A beautiful sandy coloured frame surrounds this small wooden door in one of the many courtyards of the Amer Fort, Jaipur, India.*

8

PAGE 112 *A glorious cascade of autumn colour surrounds a London door.*

PAGE 113 *Burano, Italy – an island close to Venice that boasts houses and doors painted in all the colours of the rainbow.*

OPPOSITE *The simplicity of this door is charming. The choice of bubblegum pink and forest green indicate a certain panache when it comes to colour combinations.*

ABOVE *Paris is full of secret passages, catacombs and underground tunnels. Lodged between two steep staircases in Montmartre, it's a mystery as to where this door leads or why it's there.*

PAGES 116 AND 117 *Not for the shy and retiring type: bold geometric designs demand our attention on the island of Burano, Venice.*

OPPOSITE *Foliage is often all that's needed to bring a door to life. These two examples share a striking colour palette – turquoise paintwork enlivened by fiery shades of pink and orange.*

PAGES 120 AND 121 *Humble wooden doors with an earthy rustic vibe.*

29
POSTA
Più o meno DA BRIVIDO

OPPOSITE *What catches the eye here is the cunning improvised mechanism that has replaced the door knocker: a rope attached to a bell.*

ABOVE *A passionate embrace on the streets of Funchal, Madeira.*

PAGES 124–125 *It's interesting to see what people come up with when their creativity is given free rein. Here, an elegantly coiffed mermaid contemplates the big blue alongside a map of Madeira formed from defunct computer keys.*

105

ABOVE *On Thirasia, a tiny island next to Santorini in Greece, what catches the eye is the striking symmetrical arrangement of these arched doors and windows and the perfectly harmonizing shades of blue.*

OPPOSITE *Similar hues in Essaouira, Morocco: three little doors that are almost exactly the same blue as the sky.*

PAGE 128 *It's hard to believe this French door is still in use. It has lost its windows, but serves as a porch for the main front door just behind it.*

PAGE 129 *Unassuming doors such as this one can be found all over Europe, usually set on narrow cobbled streets in small but densely populated towns.*

7

99

ABOVE *Doors that dreams are made of: Le Petit Palace in Santorini (above) and a Lebanese door (opposite).*

PAGES 132 AND 133 *Decorative door furniture brings status and a sense of purpose to these Italian doors.*

2
CASSETTA
PER
LE LETTERE

OPPOSITE *The ornate ironwork grille protecting this Italian door casts intriguing shadows.*

ABOVE *Some doors provide the perfect blank canvas. In NYC, an artist has used an entire facade to create an eye-catching entrance.*

PAGES 136 AND 137 *Ferocious felines by Peruvian street artist Meki.*

MEKI!

de.de
LIMP
RAVEDAN2
NO FACES
ALIAS

PAGES 138–139 *Ancient carved fruitwood doors from Nuristan now occupy a London garden.*

RIGHT *The city of Chefchaouen in north western Morocco is twinned with the city of Jodhpur in Rajasthan. Both are full of enchanting doors and doorways in every imaginable shade of blue.*

112

OPPOSITE AND ABOVE *Intricate detailing in the Bahia Palace, Marrakech (opposite), and graceful simplicity in the souk (above).*

PAGES 144–145 *Isola di San Pietro is an island just off the south western coast of Sardinia. The houses along the seafront of the island's only town, Carloforte, are washed in pastel shades and this is just one example – mint green with a peach and lilac trim.*

5

PAGE 146 *The medieval door of St Edward's Church in Stow-on-the-Wold in the Cotswolds is flanked by considerably older yew trees and reputed to be the inspiration for Tolkien's Doors of Durin in* The Lord of the Rings.

PAGE 147 *A painted door slowly giving itself up to encroaching foliage.*

ABOVE *One of the four imposing and majestic doors in the inner courtyard of the City Palace, Jaipur, India.*

OPPOSITE *Fez, Morocco. An intricately decorated door in the ancient Medina, home to traditional artisanal crafts including leather tanneries, metal workers and rug workshops.*

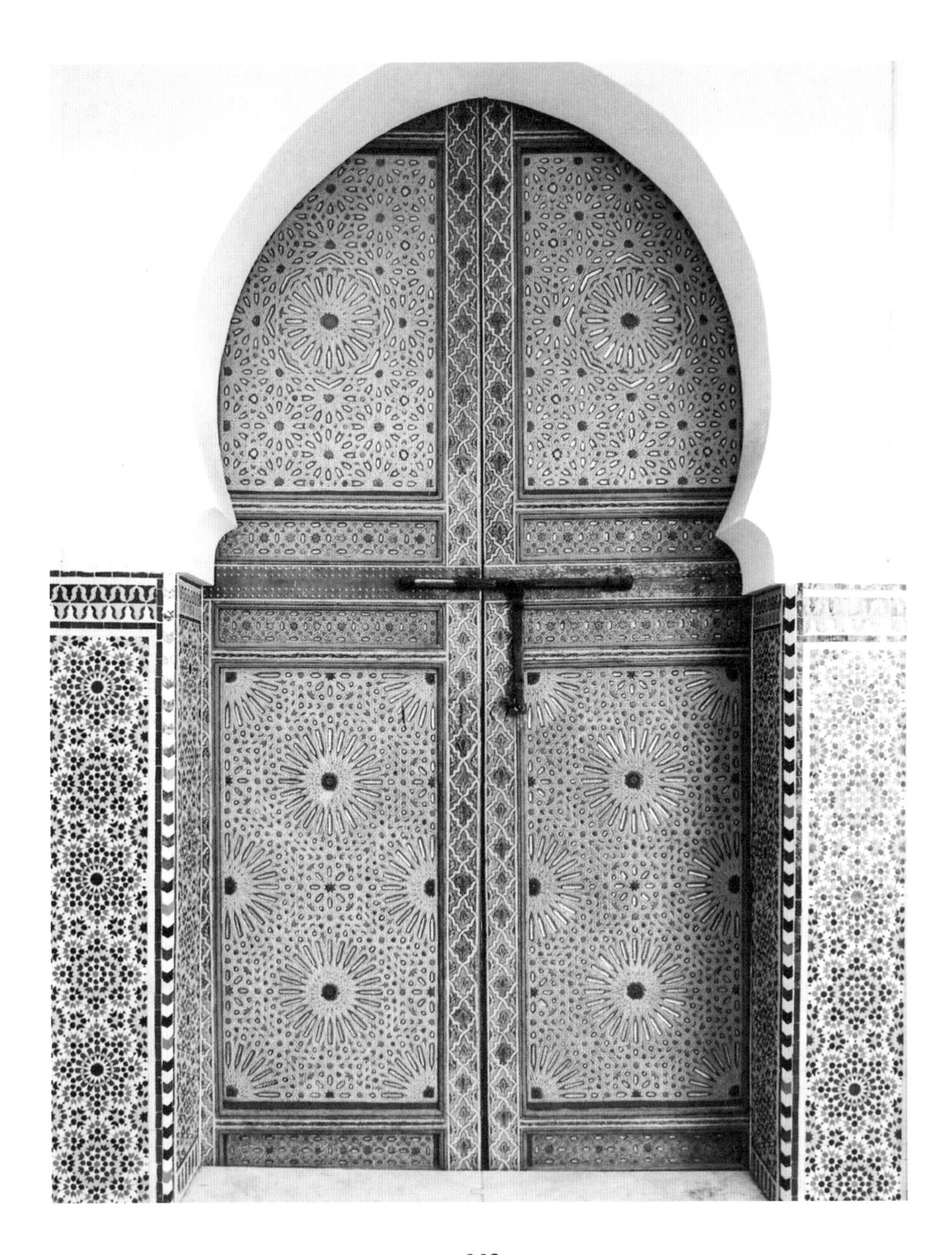

363

PAGE 150 *A pick-and-mix of different architectural details, colours and textures surround grand double doors with one left temptingly ajar.*

PAGE 151 *The candy coloured pink, white and green marble exterior of Il Duomo, Florence. A carved wooden side door is overshadowed by the elaborate, highly decorated Gothic revival façade.*

OPPOSITE *Perhaps what gives this narrow, modest door its appeal is the chalky pink of the walls that surround it.*

ABOVE *A cunning optical illusion, this charming trompe l'oeil painting completely transforms a featureless door in a wall.*

PAGE 152 *Antique Indian wooden doors with coffering studded with carved floral motifs.*

PAGE 153 *A stolen glimpse into a surrealist interior.*

61

50

8

PAGES 156 AND 157 *Alas, this imposing double door with its sunray arched fanlight looks as if it may have fallen on hard times (page 156), as does its doppelgänger in Pisa, Italy (page 157).*

OPPOSITE *Impressionist vibes on the streets of Funchal, Madeira.*

ABOVE *Those of us wanting to make our homes inviting and welcoming often go to extraordinary ends.*

PICTURE CREDITS

KEY c = centre, l = left, r = right, b = below, a = above

Endpapers Camilla Massu; **1** Nick Rowell; **2–3** José Maria Montero; **4l** Nick Rowell; **4c** Camilla Massu; **4r** @meanderingmacaron; **5** Nick Rowell; **6** Jodie Hinds; **8–9** Nick Rowell; **10–11** Jodie Hinds; **12** Nick Rowell; **13** Alexandra Lhermite-Schwass @whatalexloves; **14** Mark Scott/CICO Books; **15** Hana Yoosuf @dazzleberries; **16–17** Jeanne Salvanes; **18–19** Helen Leech; **20** Fazenda Vargem Grande, a historic coffee plantation in the Paraiba Valley restored by Clemente Fagundes Gomes with gardens by Roberto Burle Marx, ph. Maíra Acayaba/© Ryland Peters & Small; **21** Steve Painter/© Ryland Peters & Small **22–23** Nick Rowell; **24–25** Jodie Hinds; **26** The home of Tad Wilbur in Co. Sligo, ph. James Fennell/© Ryland Peters & Small; **27** Mathilde Crolais; **28–29** Jodie Hinds; **30** Yannis Papadimitrou; **31** Julia Fougstedt; **32** Helen Leech; **33** Alexandra Lhermite-Schwass @whatalexloves; **34–35** Nick Rowell; **36** José Maria Montero; **37** Louisa Wells; **38–39** Camilla Massu; **40** Jodie Hinds; **41** Venetia Stanley; **42** Alexandra Lhermite-Schwass @whatalexloves; **43** The home of Susan Callery, owner of Greenlane Gallery, in Dingle (www.greenlanegallery.com), ph. James Fennell/© Ryland Peters & Small; **44–45** José Maria Montero; **46** Venetia Stanley; **47** Nick Rowell/Ben Westaway; **48** A house in Provence designed by architect Alexandre Lafourcade www.architecture-lafourcade.com, ph. Jan Baldwin/© Ryland Peters & Small; **49** Malcolm Gliksten's home in France, ph. Claire Richardson/© Ryland Peters & Small; **50–51** Camilla Massu; **52** Jay Kim; **53** Alex Kennedy; **54–56** Nick Rowell; **57** Helen Leech; **58–59** José Maria Montero; **60–61** Jodie Hinds; **62** Nick Rowell; **63** Camilla Massu; **64** Simon Brown/ CICO Books; **65** Matthew and Miranda Eden's home in Wiltshire, ph. Chris Tubbs/© Ryland Peters & Small; **66** Alice Alias; **67** José Maria Montero; **68** Amanjena Resort @sarahirenemurphy; **69** Lis Huang; **70–71** Venetia Willis; **72–73** José Maria Montero; **74al** Nick Rowell; **74ar** Camilla Massu; **74br** and **75** Jodie Hinds; **74bl** Alex Alias; **76** Helen Leech; **77** Oleg Znamenskiy; **78–79** José Maria Montero; **80** Venetia Stanley; **81** Camilla Massu; **82** Alexandra Lhermite-Schwass @whatalexloves; **83–84** Nick Rowell; **85** Victoria Desailly Y Marcus Thouant; **86–87** falko1; **88** Claire Richardson/© Ryland Peters & Small; **89** The summer home of Ritva Puotila in Finland, ph. Paul Ryan/© Ryland Peters & Small; **90** Helen Leech; **91** Nick Rowell; **92–93** falko1; **94** Clare McCelland; **95** Alexandra Lhermite-Schwass @whatalexloves; **96** Nick Rowell; **97** Lola Roux; **98–99** José Maria Montero; **100** Camilla Massu; **101–103** Nick Rowell; **104** Francesca Gentili; **105** Helen Leech; **106–107** Camilla Massu; **108–109** Nick Rowell; **110–111** Camilla Massu; **112** @meanderingmacaron; **113** Jodie Hinds; **114–115** Nick Rowell; **116** Jodie Hinds; **117** John Hutchins; **118** Jemma Neville; **119** Kelsey Hennegen; **120** From *Imperfect Home* by Mark and Sally Bailey. www.starnet-bkds.com. ph Debi Treloar/© Ryland Peters & Small; **121** The home of Charmaine and Paul Jack in Belvezet, France, ph Claire Richardson/ © Ryland Peters & Small; **122** Nick Rowell; **123** José Maria Montero; **124–125** José Maria Montero; **126** Tom Dempsey; **127** Alexandra Lhermite-Schwass @whatalexloves; **128–129** Nick Rowell; **130** Le Petit Palace Hotel, Santorini; **131** Charbel Fersan; **132–133** Nick Rowell; **134** Jodie Hinds; **135** Camilla Massu; **136–137** Christian Rowell; **138–139** From *Imperfect Home* by Mark and Sally Bailey. www.piprau.com, ph Debi Treloar/© Ryland Peters & Small; **140–141** Alexandra Lhermite-Schwass @whatalexloves; **142–143** Peter Cassidy/© Ryland Peters & Small; **144–145** Nick Rowell; **146** Jethro Lyne; **147** Nick Rowell; **148** Venetia Stanley; **149** Alexandra Lhermite-Schwass @whatalexloves; **150–151** Helen Leech; **152** Nick Rowell; **153** Christian Rowell; **154** Richard Boll/© CICO Books; **155** José Maria Montero; **156–157** Nick Rowell; **158** José Maria Montero; **159** Camilla Massu

ACKNOWLEDGMENTS

The first people to acknowledge are those who contributed enormously to this book and share my passion for doors: Camilla Massu, Alexandre Alias, José Maria Montero, Helen Leech, Jodi Hinds and Alexandra Lhermite-Schwass. Thanks to Ryland Peters & Small, in particular Annabel Morgan, Cindy Richards, Leslie Harrington and Toni Kay, who also believe in the beauty of doors. Thanks to my friends – who probably hate doors now – for supporting this idea: Gabs, Vinay, Walker, Tash, Jacob, Giada, Roz, Paul, Sami, Tom, Vincent, Vic, Cus, Doudou, CA, Dunc, PO, Venetia, Jamie, Ben, Soph and Neo. And most of all, thanks to my family, to whom I dedicate this book: Maman et Papa, David, Anne, Bill and Lucy.